Dolly's Kindness Journey

Written by
Melissa Eastin

Illustrated by
Lana Lee

Listen closely to this tale just for you,
a lesson of **kindness** and **friendship** too.

Starring Dolly,

spreading good deeds and cheer.

Snuggle close little one, for her lesson is dear.

Dolly the Doodle is a playful pretty pup, with her **big dreams**, she never seems to give up.

In a world full of wonders, she loves to explore.
An adventure awaits, with new friends and more!

Bounding out the door
for her morning walkabout,
she stumbles upon something
and gives it a snout.

A mysterious box wrapped
with a big yellow bow,
sparkling in the sunshine
with a shimmering glow.

With a wag of her tail and a curious **grin**, she quickly opens the box and peeks right in.

Inside lay a trail map, colorful and bright.
There's an important message, **full of delight!**

Excited she bounces along the adventurous trail,

through meadows and forests,

with a happy wagging tail.

You see, the map has a mission
to help friends in need.

Find the mystery letters on the map.

Can you help her make
the kind choices to succeed?

First, she meets Sami, a silly sloth stranded up high,
struggling to reach a ripe red apple way up in the sky.
A quick whip of her dazzling
doodle lasso saves the day.
She ropes Sami down from
the tree and soon is on her way.

Reader's Choice

Help Dolly make a kind choice. What should she do?

A. Share the apple with Sami; what a tasty treat.

B. Keep the apple for herself, so delicious to eat.

Together, they share the apple
so juicy to eat.
Laughing in the sunshine,
the time couldn't be beat.

The map leads her to a new friend,
the very best find.
A friendship blossoms by
truly helping and **being kind**.

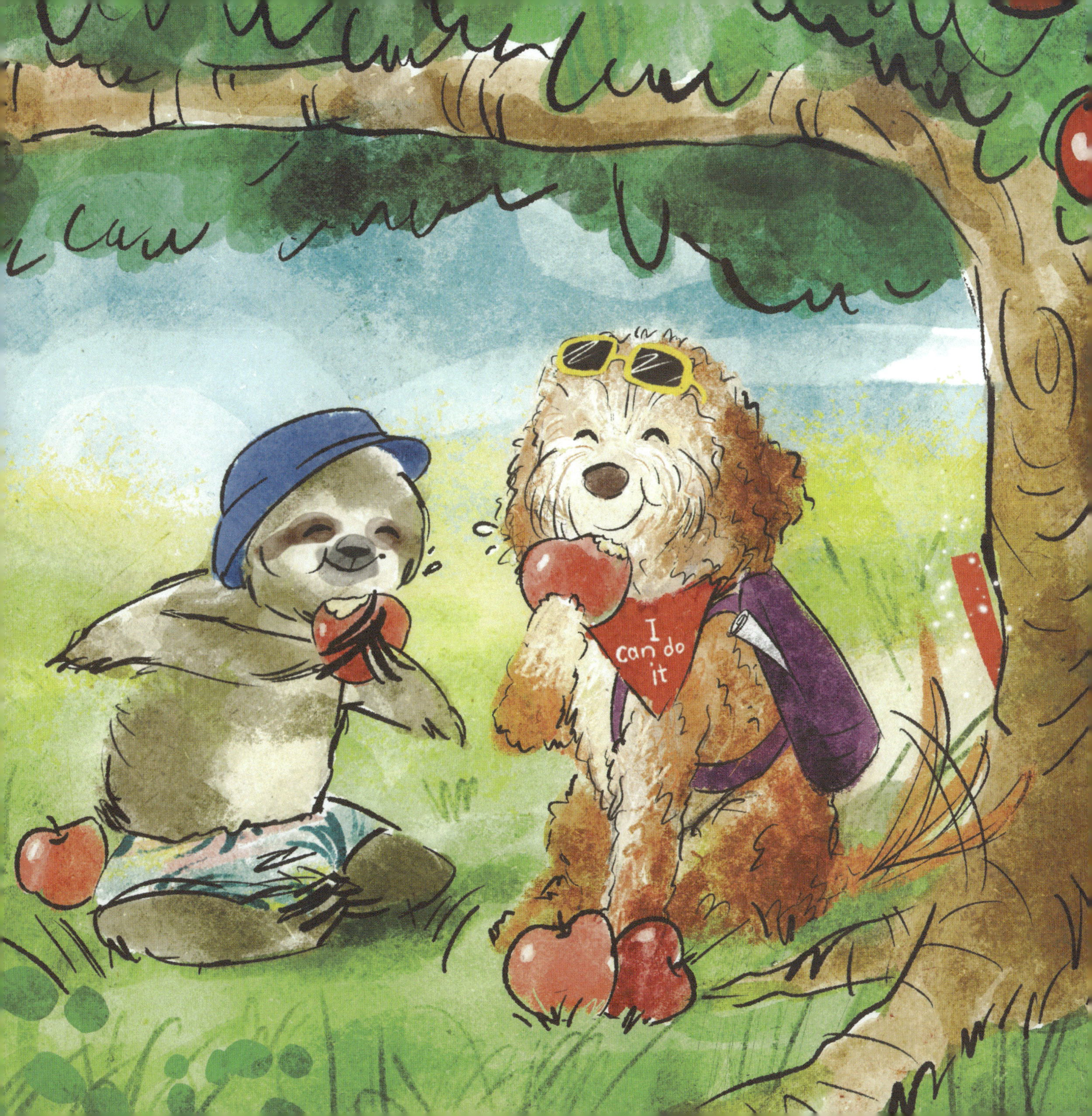
I can do it

Dolly prances and grins, feeling full of glee.
Helping others is awesome, as you can see!

Dolly sings sweetly,

Let's Sing Along!

"**Kindness** is a **gift** for all to **share**,
Your simple acts of **kindness** show others **you** do **care**."

In a playful pounce, she finds a shy little fawn,

feeling quite nervous,
his confidence was nearly gone.

With a dilly doodle dance, Dolly makes him smile.
Dolly lends a listening ear as they play for a while.

Reader's Choice

Help Dolly make a kind choice. What should she do?

A. Listen to Finley the Fawn and help him feel better. Invite him on the quest.

B. Continue on the journey and don't worry about Finley. He'll feel better after rest.

Together, they follow the map's **kindness** quest.
Dolly and Finley, always striving for their best.

Spreading lots of happiness along the trail
and helping others along the way, they do prevail!

As they were exploring,
 with the mysterious map in hand,
they stumble across a yellow duckling
 crying in the sand.

Lost and scared and
 too little to be left all alone,
she surely needs some help,
 finding her way back home.

Reader's Choice

Help Dolly and Finely make a kind choice. What should they do?

A. Help the lost duckling find her way back home.
B. Say goodbye to the little duck and let her roam.

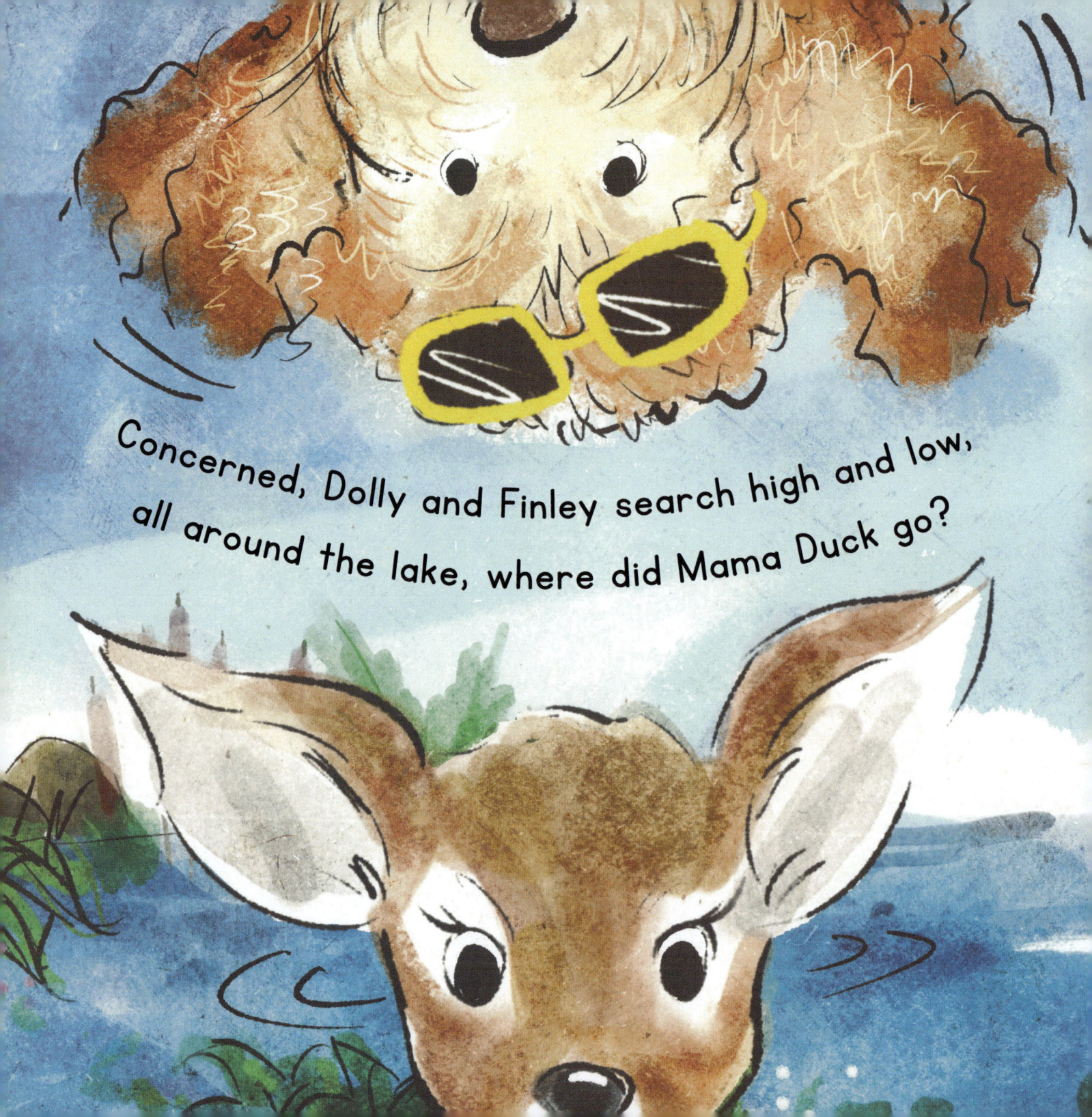

Concerned, Dolly and Finley search high and low, all around the lake, where did Mama Duck go?

Nowhere to be found,
the three friends venture on their way.
Together, with a woof, snort, quack,
and lots of silly play.

Through the journey's challenge,
the friends face a steep, steep crest.
A narrow bridge needs crossing,
putting **courage** to the test.

Finley shakes in fear because to cross
he must **brave** the height.
One wobbly step at a time,
he tiptoes slowly with fright.

Reader's Choice

Help Dolly make a kind choice. What should she do?

A. Hold Finley's hand and help him along the way.
B. Give up on the mission and choose to stay.

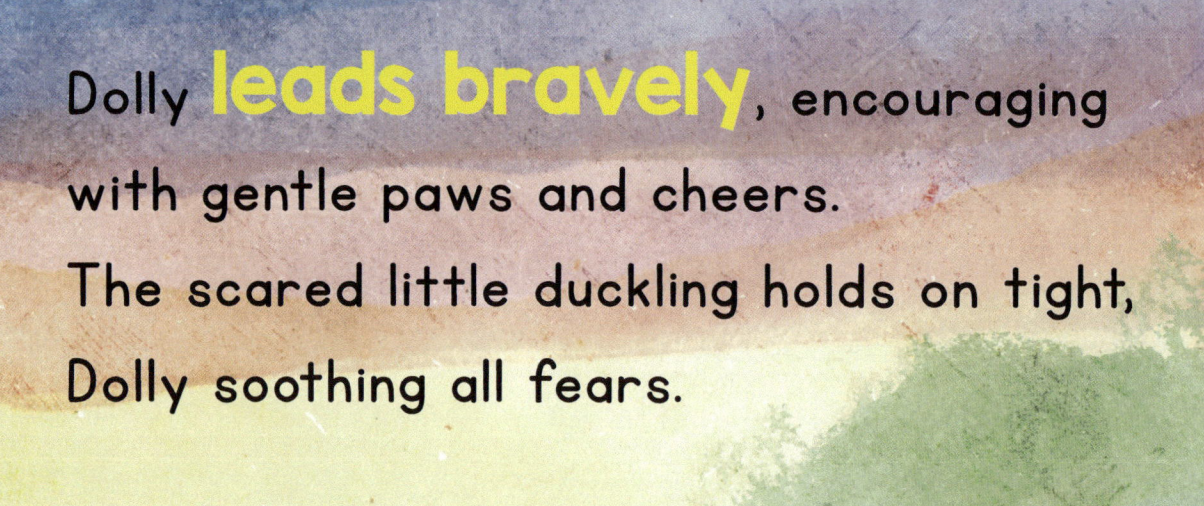

Dolly **leads bravely**, encouraging with gentle paws and cheers.
The scared little duckling holds on tight, Dolly soothing all fears.

The friends tread hand in hand across the quite narrow bridge.
Teamwork in action, they cross over the terrifying ridge!

"You can do it!"

Finley, with his newfound **confidence**,
has a clever thought.
He exclaims, "Under the bridge,
the map shows the spot!"

They quickly run down the hill
and find a surprise.
There huddling is Mother Duck
with her **grateful** eyes.

At last, Duckling is home safely,
and Dolly smiles with glee.
Helping others is awesome,
as you can see!

Dolly sings sweetly,

"**Kindness** is a **gift** for all to **share**,
Your simple acts of **kindness** show others **you** do **care**."

Dolly and Finley celebrate, their task now complete.
Hungry and tired, they share an ice cream treat.

So, refreshing and sweet,
like a new best friend,
promising the **kindness**
journey will never end.

So, little one, always remember Dolly's grand day,
and the important message the tale does say.

KINDNESS

With simple acts of **kindness**,
both big and small,
You'll change the world
– a joyful lesson for all!

"Let us remember: One book, one pen, one child, and one teacher can change the world."

Malala Yousafzai

Copyright © Dolly's Adventure 2023 All rights reserved.

No part of this book may be duplicated without permission.

Discussion Questions:
Preschool and Kindergarten (Ages 3-6)

Kindness and Friendship:
- What did the characters in the story do to show kindness to each other?
- Can you think of a time when you were kind to someone like the characters in the book?
- How will you show kindness today?

Identifying Emotions:
- How do you think the main character felt when (specific event in the book) happened?
- Can you show me a face that expresses that feeling?

Empathy and Understanding Others:
- Why do you think the character felt sad/happy/angry in that part of the story (share an event)?
- How would you help a friend who is feeling the same way?

Problem-Solving:
- What could the characters have done differently when they faced a problem in the story?
- Can you think of another way they could have solved it?

Cooperation and Teamwork:
- When did the characters work together in the story? How did that help them?
- Can you and a friend pretend to be the characters and solve a problem together?

Discussion Questions:
Grades 1-2 (Ages 6-8)

Resolving Conflicts:
- What were the main conflicts in the story, and how did the characters solve them?

Applying Lessons Learned:
- What lessons did the characters learn in the story? How can you apply those lessons in your own life?
- Can you tell me about a time when you used something you learned from a story to help yourself or someone else?
- How will you show kindness today?

Interactive Activities:
- Role-Play Scenarios: Divide kids into groups and assign different scenes from the book to act out. Encourage them to consider the characters' emotions and reactions.- How would you help a friend who is feeling the same way?
- Create a Kindness Poster: Have the children create a poster showcasing acts of kindness they can do in school or at home.

These questions and activities aim to spark discussions and engage children in activities that promote kindness, empathy, emotional understanding, and problem-solving based on the themes of the book.

About the Author

Melissa Eastin, M.Ed., creator of the beloved Dolly the Doodle Adventures Series, is a devoted mother, experienced educator with 28 years in the classroom, and a passionate advocate for children's social-emotional development. Drawing inspiration from her enthusiastic dog Chloe, Melissa introduces essential life skills through Dolly's relatable adventures. Her mission is to empower young readers with confidence and empathy, making her books a valuable resource for parents, teachers, and counselors alike.
Connect with Melissa: www.positivepawsreading.com

Please Leave Us a Review: Your voice truly matters. If you enjoyed this book, It would mean the world to me, if you would drop a short review on Amazon. Your kind feedback is very important and appreciated. Thank you for your time.

About the Illustrator

Lana Lee is a passionate children's book illustrator who loves to hear the story from the author and bring it to life through her drawings. She has been creating art since she was a child and her unique illustrations have a talent for making stories come alive. You can check out her work at https://imlanalee.com and contact her at imlanalee@gmail.com.

Dolly's Adventure SERIES

We'd love it if you left us a review!

www.positivepawsreading.com

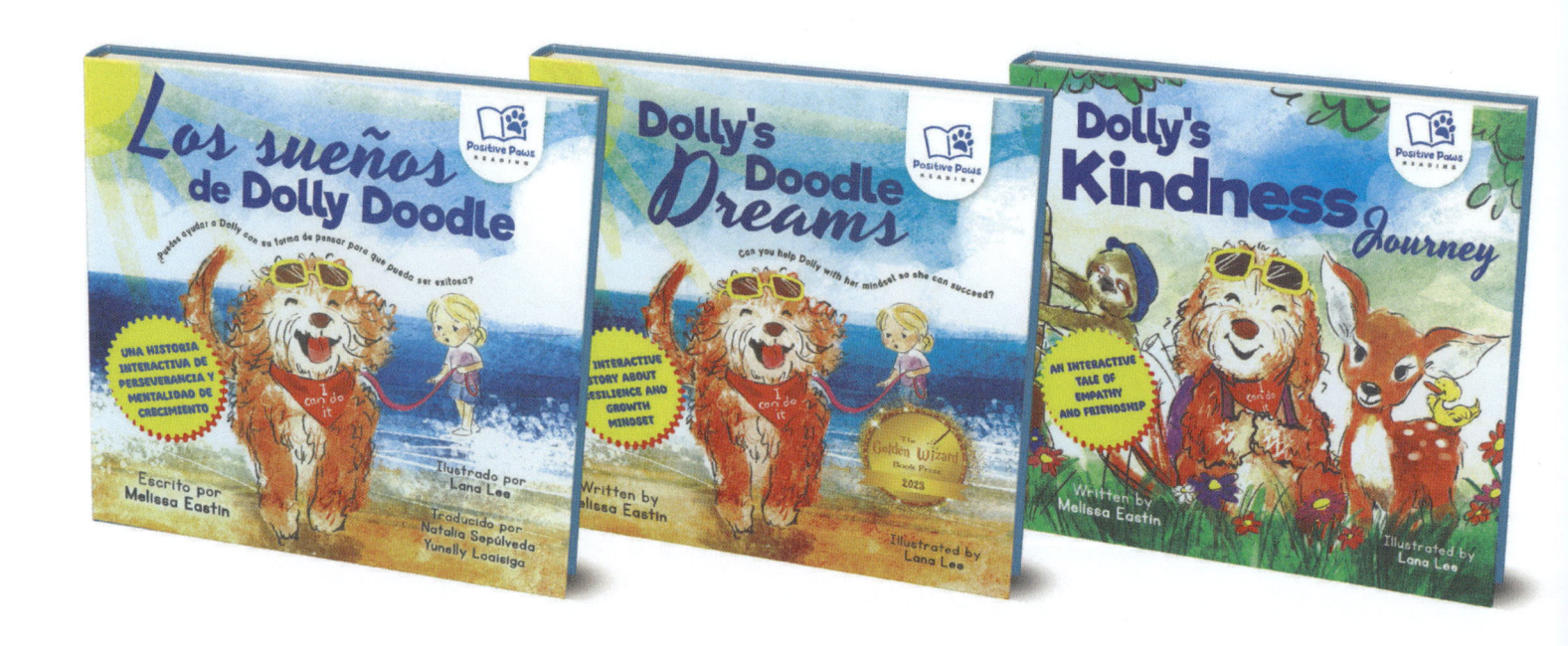

Printed in Great Britain
by Amazon